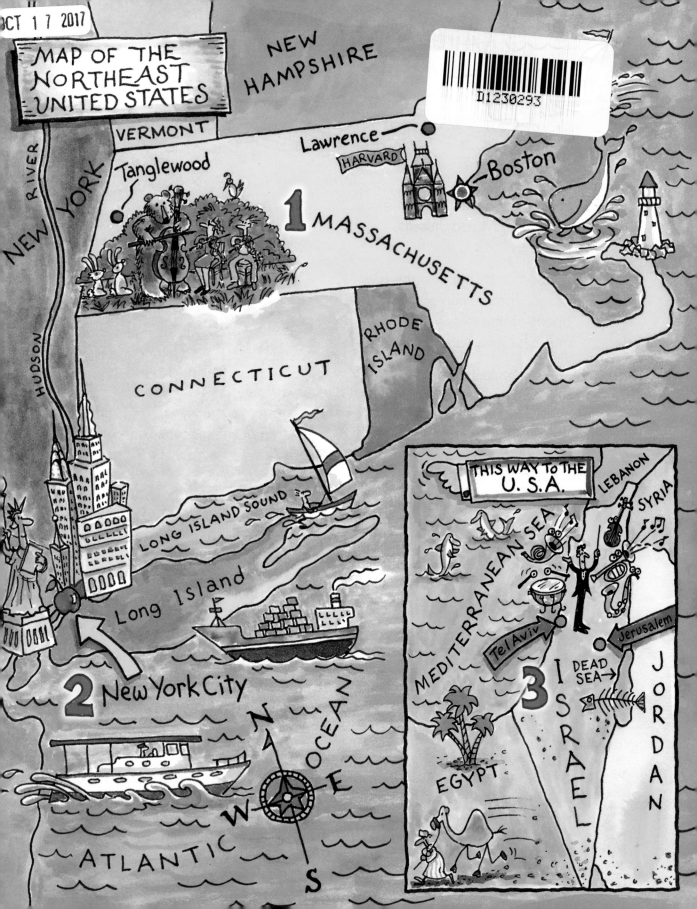

TIMELINE OF LEONARD BERNSTEIN'S LIFE

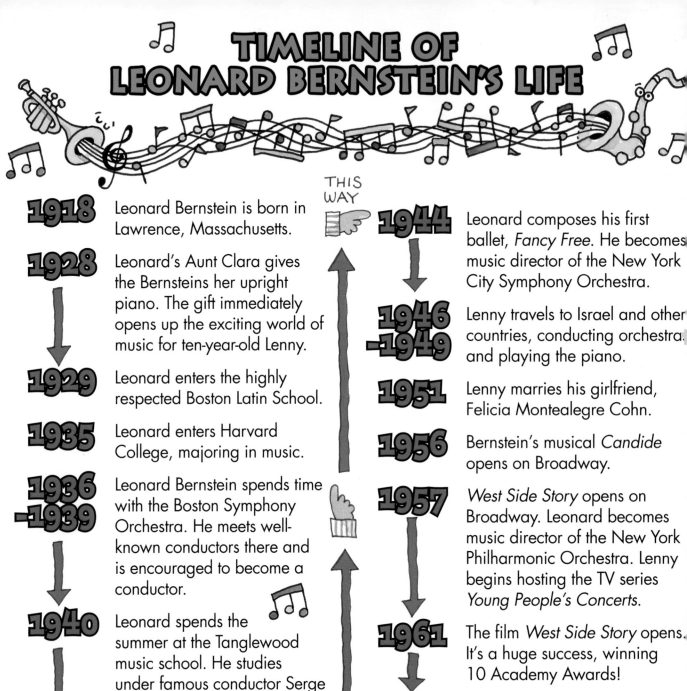

THIS WAY

1918 Leonard Bernstein is born in Lawrence, Massachusetts.

1928 Leonard's Aunt Clara gives the Bernsteins her upright piano. The gift immediately opens up the exciting world of music for ten-year-old Lenny.

1929 Leonard enters the highly respected Boston Latin School.

1935 Leonard enters Harvard College, majoring in music.

1936 –1939 Leonard Bernstein spends time with the Boston Symphony Orchestra. He meets well-known conductors there and is encouraged to become a conductor.

1940 Leonard spends the summer at the Tanglewood music school. He studies under famous conductor Serge Koussevitzky.

1942 Leonard moves to New York City. The next year, he makes a spectacular appearance at Carnegie Hall when the regular conductor becomes ill.

1944 Leonard composes his first ballet, *Fancy Free*. He becomes music director of the New York City Symphony Orchestra.

1946 –1949 Lenny travels to Israel and other countries, conducting orchestras and playing the piano.

1951 Lenny marries his girlfriend, Felicia Montealegre Cohn.

1956 Bernstein's musical *Candide* opens on Broadway.

1957 *West Side Story* opens on Broadway. Leonard becomes music director of the New York Philharmonic Orchestra. Lenny begins hosting the TV series *Young People's Concerts*.

1961 The film *West Side Story* opens. It's a huge success, winning 10 Academy Awards!

1969 –1989 Leonard continues conducting, composing, and playing piano around the world.

1990 Leonard Bernstein conducts his last concert. He dies in New York on October 14.

UP HERE

GETTING TO KNOW
THE WORLD'S
GREATEST COMPOSERS

LEONARD BERNSTEIN

WRITTEN AND ILLUSTRATED BY MIKE VENEZIA

CONSULTANT
DONALD FREUND, PROFESSOR OF COMPOSITION,
INDIANA UNIVERSITY SCHOOL OF MUSIC

CHILDREN'S PRESS®

An Imprint of Scholastic Inc.

Dedicated to the memory of my mother, Patricia Venezia, with love.

Picture Acknowledgements
Music on the cover, Stock Montage, Inc.; 3, The Bettmann Archive; 5, Victor Haboush; 11, AP/
Photographs ©: Stock Montage, Inc.: Music on the cover and title page; Archive Photos: 3;
Art Resource: 6 top; Photofest: 6 bottom (Courtesy of the Estate of Leonard Bernstein); Art
Resource: 7; Victor Haboush: 8; Corbis-Bettmann: 12; Balkin: 15; William P. Gottlieb: 15 inset,
16; The New York Times, NYT Pictures: 20; William P. Gottlieb: 22 top; Corbis-Bettmann: 22
bottom; The Kobal Collection: 24; Shooting Star International Photo Agency: 24 top inset; The
Kobal Collection: 25; Shooting Start International Photo Agency: 26, 27, 27; Corbis-Bettmann:
32 center; UPI/Corbis-Bettmann: 32 bottom.

Library of Congress Cataloging-in-Publication Data

Names: Venezia, Mike, author, illustrator.
Title: Leonard Bernstein / written and illustrated by Mike Venezia.
Description: Revised edition. | New York : Children's Press, 2017. | Series:
   Getting to know the world's greatest composers | Includes bibliographical
   references and index.
Identifiers: LCCN 2017022725| ISBN 9780531226568 (library binding : alk.
   paper) | ISBN 9780531230343 (pbk. : alk. paper)
Subjects: LCSH: Bernstein, Leonard, 1918-1990--Juvenile literature. |
   Musicians--United States--Biography--Juvenile literature.
Classification: LCC ML3930.B48 V46 2017 | DDC 780.92 [B] --dc23 LC record available at
   https://lccn.loc.gov/2017022725

1 2 3 4 5 6 7 8 9 10 R 27 26 25 24 23 22 21 20 19 18

Leonard Bernstein loved teaching young people about the joy of music.

Leonard Bernstein was born in Lawrence, Massachusetts, in 1918. He not only composed music, but was known as a great conductor and pianist. Leonard Bernstein also spent much of his time teaching children and adults about the joy of music.

Some people thought that composing, conducting, playing the piano, and teaching were too much for any one person to do all at once. They thought Leonard Bernstein would be better off if he concentrated on one area of music so that he could do it really well. But Leonard loved every area of music so

much that he couldn't help it. He ended
up surprising people by doing everything
very well.

Leonard Bernstein thought all kinds
of music were equally beautiful and
important. He got as much enjoyment from
good rock, jazz, folk, or religious music as
he got from a Beethoven symphony.

While growing up, Leonard Bernstein learned that music is an important part of Jewish tradition. This painting shows a traditional Jewish wedding in Eastern Europe.

Leonard Bernstein grew up in a Jewish family where religion was very important. The Bernsteins believed that worship is a joyful event and that music should be a big part of that experience. Members of their synagogue often sang, clapped, and danced as a way of honoring God.

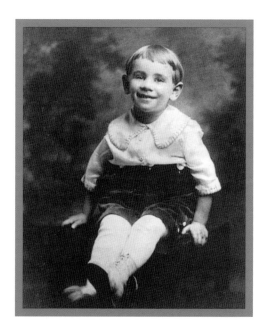

Leonard at the age of two

Leonard grew up listening to traditional Jewish melodies. He was fascinated by the sound of the powerful organ that accompanied the singers at his synagogue. Sometimes people there acted out stories from the Bible. At an early age, Leonard saw how stories could be told with words and music.

Leonard was influenced by other music, too. In the 1920s, when he was growing up, people all over the United States were beginning to get radios in their homes. Leonard enjoyed listening to the exciting rhythms and loud, brassy sounds of popular jazz and boogie-woogie music.

A painting by Victor Haboush of Leonard listening to the radio as a child

When he was ten years old, something happened that changed Leonard Bernstein's life forever. His aunt Clara decided to move, and she asked if she could store her piano at the Bernsteins' house. The moment Leonard saw the piano and played his first note, he found himself hooked on music forever.

Leonard began taking piano lessons right away. He was an excellent student, and he usually ended up knowing more than his teachers did after a short time. Luckily, the Bernsteins lived very close to Boston, Massachusetts, which was a great music city. It was easy for Leonard to find the best teachers while he was growing up.

Leonard also found it was easy to go to the famous Boston Symphony Orchestra concerts. Since he and his friends didn't have much money, they would sit way high up in the back of the concert hall, where the seats were less expensive. Even though the orchestra seemed miles away, Leonard couldn't wait for that magical moment when the lights went down and the conductor appeared.

The Boston Symphony Orchestra in the 1930s

At that time, the Boston Symphony Orchestra was led by one of the greatest conductors in the world, Serge Koussevitzky. Listening to Koussevitzky direct the orchestra, Leonard had no idea that someday he and the great conductor would become very best friends.

Serge Koussevitzky

During his teenage years, Leonard became an excellent pianist. He played every chance he got, whether it was in school symphony orchestras, jazz clubs, or at a friend's party. He often showed up at a party and played nonstop from the moment he got there until the party was over. Some of his friends said they never remembered seeing Leonard Bernstein away from a piano.

Leonard Bernstein was also becoming interested in composing music and conducting. When he found out that Serge Koussevitzky was starting a music school in Tanglewood, Massachusetts, Leonard jumped at the chance to join up. At the Berkshire Music Center in Tanglewood, Leonard got to meet his idol and learn important lessons about conducting from him. Leonard also studied piano and composing.

Serge taught his students that the conductor's most important job is to figure out exactly what composers had in mind and what they were feeling when they wrote music. Then the conductor has to get the orchestra to play that music just right, so that people listening can get the most joy out of it. Serge believed that Leonard Bernstein was one of the few people who could do this well. He worked hard with Leonard to develop this special talent.

Opposite page: Leonard practicing piano (bottom) and working with Serge Koussevitzky (top)

Leonard conducting a rehearsal during his early years with the New York Philharmonic

When Leonard Bernstein was 25 years old, he was asked to be the assistant conductor of the New York Philharmonic Orchestra. Being an assistant conductor didn't give Leonard much of a chance to conduct, but he was happy to have the job. Leonard mostly helped out with a lot of boring things that the regular conductor was too busy to do.

Leonard was always prepared, though, in case he was ever called upon to conduct at the last minute. He carefully studied all the music that the orchestra played, bought a tuxedo, and even rented an apartment over the concert hall so that he could be ready at a moment's notice.

Finally, his hard work, talent, and planning paid off. Shortly before a big performance, the world-famous guest conductor, Bruno Walter, got sick with the flu. This was a special performance, too, because it was going to be broadcast live

on radio all over the United States. Leonard was called in to take over. He was so nervous he was shaking like crazy.

When he heard the disappointed audience moan and groan as his name was announced, it made him a little angry. As he walked out on the stage, Leonard gained confidence, and he made up his mind to show everyone that he could do the job.

19

Leonard is congratulated by members of the New York Philharmonic Orchestra right after his triumphant debut.

Leonard Bernstein did exactly what he had hoped to do. Everyone was surprised! Not only did he do a good job, but Leonard directed the orchestra to play the music in a more exciting and beautiful way than anyone ever expected. At the end of the concert, the audience applauded and cheered over and over again. Most people thought he did a better job than Bruno Walter would have done. The next day there were stories in newspapers across the country about Leonard's great performance. Overnight, Leonard Bernstein was famous!

Soon Leonard was getting tons of offers to be a guest conductor from lots of different orchestras. He was very busy and very happy. He hoped that an important orchestra would ask him to be their full-time conductor. While he was waiting for that to happen, Leonard got even busier by composing music. He wrote music for Broadway plays, symphonies, and ballets. Leonard enjoyed writing music as much as he enjoyed conducting.

Bernstein composing music (above) and conducting while playing the piano during a rehearsal (right)

He usually worked very quickly, writing down page after page of musical notes. Once he stopped in the middle of a page to tell a friend how exciting it was to be able to hear in his head the music that comes out of all the little black dots!

In 1944, Leonard Bernstein had his first big Broadway hit. It was a musical comedy called *On the Town*. It was about three sailors who try to jam in as much fun as they can while they're in New York City on their day off. The music Leonard wrote goes perfectly with the happy adventures the sailors had in New York.

Leonard Bernstein loved New York City. He composed music for other plays, ballets, and even a movie that took place there. He became best known for the musical play *West Side Story*, which he wrote in 1957.

Scenes from the movie *On the Town*

A scene of tension between the two street gangs in the movie *West Side Story*

In *West Side Story*, Bernstein captured just the right feeling of New York's busy streets, energy, and fun, as well as the sadness and danger that can sometimes be found there.

Unlike other musicals Leonard worked on, *West Side Story* isn't a comedy at all. Even though it has some really fun songs, it's a more serious story. It's about two street gangs and what happens when a boy and girl from opposite sides fall in love. In fact, it's really an updated version of William Shakespeare's famous play *Romeo and Juliet*.

Tony and Maria, the characters who fall in love in *West Side Story*

Bernstein liked to borrow from lots of different musical traditions. The song "America," from *West Side Story*, uses Latin-American rhythms.

Leonard Bernstein often blended different music styles in his compositions. In *West Side Story* and another one of his musicals, *Candide*, you can hear everything from cool jazz to beautiful opera singing. He included the wild beat of Latin-American music, as well as circus-like comedy music.

Bernstein often mixed these with big symphonic orchestra sounds. By combining the music that influenced him while he was growing up with popular music of the day, he created a special style of all-American music that audiences loved.

Leonard (at piano) composing music with his friends Jerome Robbins, Betty Comden, and Adolph Green in 1944

Leonard Bernstein always tried to help people understand the mysteries of music. He felt that sometimes people don't like a certain composer's work because they don't understand what the composer was trying to do, or what feeling the composer was trying to create.

Leonard teaches his audience about traditional Japanese gagaku music during a televised *Young People's Concert* in the 1960s.

Leonard talks about how to read music during a televised *Young People's Concert*.

Bernstein took the time to explain all kinds of music to people so that they could get the most enjoyment out of it. In the 1950s, when television first became popular, Leonard went to work right away putting on television shows that taught children and adults how much fun and how beautiful all kinds of music can be.

Leonard Bernstein served as conductor of the New York Philharmonic from 1958 to 1969. He will long be remembered for his passionate conducting.

When Leonard Bernstein died in 1990, he had probably done more than anyone ever did to get people all over the world interested in music. Whether it was by teaching, composing, or conducting someone else's music, he helped make music more exciting and fun for everyone.

It's easy to find Leonard Bernstein's music online for free. You can also find online video clips from his television series *Young People's Concerts*.

LEARN MORE BY TAKING THE BERNSTEIN QUIZ!

(ANSWERS ON THE NEXT PAGE.)

1. When a young Leonard Bernstein was becoming interested in a music career, his father didn't agree with his choice. Instead, Mr. Bernstein encouraged Lenny to become:
- **a** A beauty-supply salesman
- **b** A plumber
- **c** A jockey

2. **TRUE OR FALSE:**
Leonard Bernstein was pretty snobby. He liked to play and conduct only serious classical music. He thought all other music was a waste of time.

3. **TRUE OR FALSE:**
Aside from being an expert on music, Leonard Bernstein was a leading authority on the history of Rybernia, a tiny music-loving country. He studied Rybernian customs and could speak the Rybernian language perfectly.

4. **TRUE OR FALSE:**
In order to become the best musician, composer, and conductor he could be, Lenny spent years studying in the great music cities of Europe, including Salzburg, Berlin, Milan, Paris, London and Moscow.

5. Leonard Bernstein was super-talented in many areas of music. But the one thing he loved to do the most was:
- **a** Conduct the orchestra
- **b** Compose music
- **c** Play the piano in concerts
- **d** Teach
- **e** Write books

ANSWERS

1. **a** Leonard's father, Sam Bernstein, owned a beauty-supply business. He wished his son would join him because he thought Lenny would never make a living as a musician. Years later, when his son had become very successful, a proud Sam told people, "Well, how was I supposed to know my son was Leonard Bernstein?"

2. **FALSE** Leonard Bernstein loved all kinds of music, from all over the world. He was crazy about jazz, folk, African, Latin American, religious, and rock-and-roll music. When teaching kids about music, he would often refer to music of the Beatles and other popular rock groups to make an important point.

3. **TRUE** Lenny could speak Rybernian perfectly. But the truth is that Rybernia wasn't a real country! As a teenager, Lenny and his friend, Eddy Ryack, invented Rybernia for fun and created an entire language! Leonard always loved learning languages and could communicate well with musicians almost anywhere in the world.

4. **FALSE** Unlike most American composers and conductors at the time, Leonard Bernstein never studied music in Europe. He found everything he needed for inspiration right at home in the United States. Probably more than any other person, Lenny brought world attention to America's musicians, composers, and conductors.

5. **d** What Leonard Bernstein loved to do the most was teach! He loved to teach people not only about music, but also anything he was interested in, such as history, astrophysics, sports, religion, and the writings of famous authors. Once he became excited about a subject, he couldn't wait to share his discoveries with others.